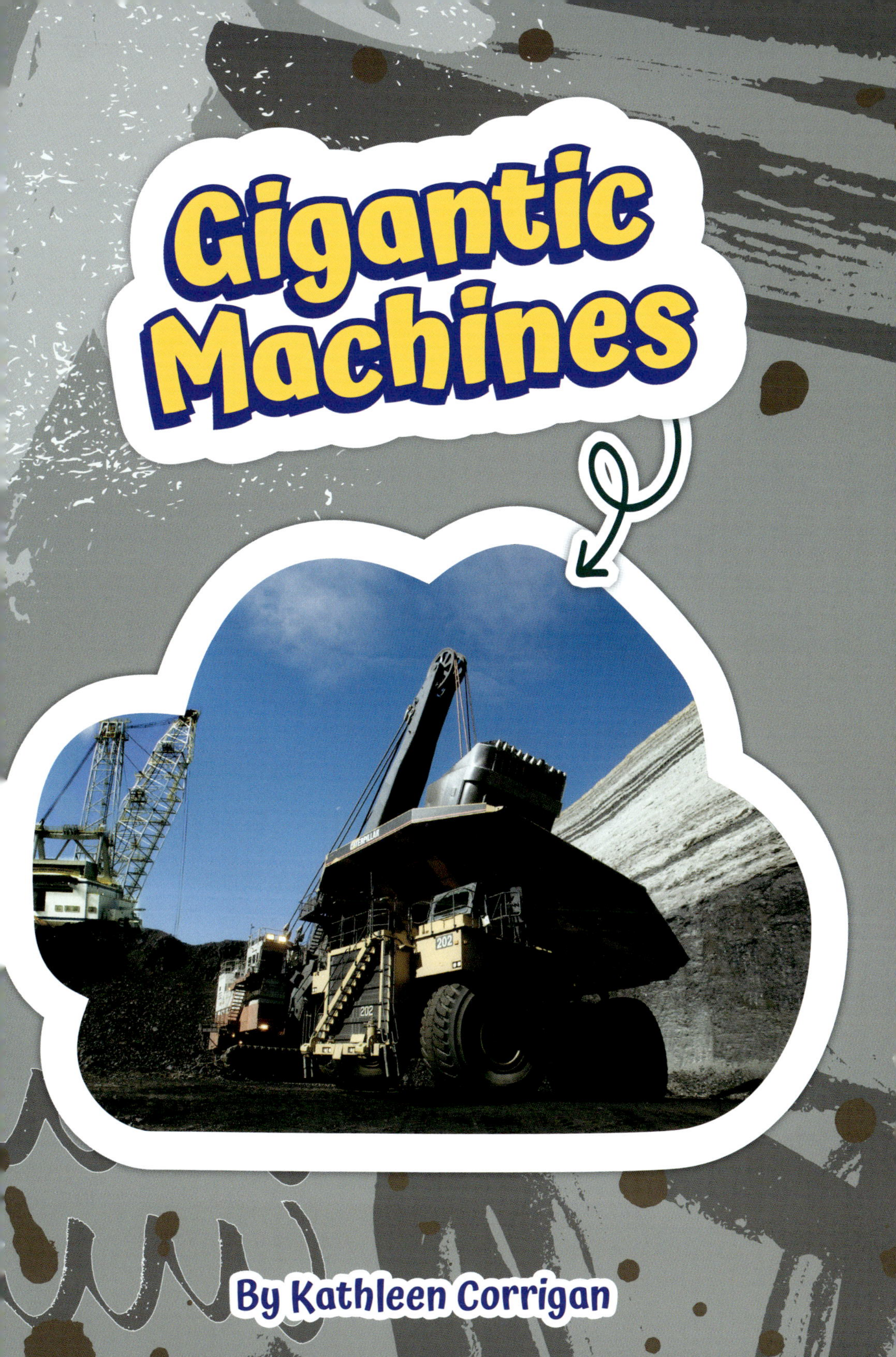
Gigantic Machines
By Kathleen Corrigan

Published by The Child's World®
800-599-READ • childsworld.com

Photography Credits
Peabody Energy, Inc./Wikimedia Commons, cover, title page, 12-13; Anna Pasichnyk/Shutterstock.com, 5, 29 (top left); Stefan Fussan/Wikimedia Commons, 7, 29 (top right); Seattle City Council/Wikimedia Commons, 9; Jani-Markus Häsä/Alamy.com, 11, 29 (bottom left); KSC/NASA, 14-15; Ruud Kaland/Shutterstock.com, 17; D-VISIONS/Shutterstock.com, 18-19, 30-31; 24K-Production/Shutterstock.com, 21 (top); NASA, 21 (bottom); Dragan Mujan/Shutterstock.com, 23, 29 (bottom right); Rube Goldberg/Wikimedia Commons, 27

ISBN Information
9781503877863 (Reinforced Library Binding)
9781503878501 (Portable Document Format)
9781503879041 (Online Multi-user eBook)
9781503879584 (Electronic Publication)

LCCN
2025938211

Printed in the United States of America

ABOUT THE AUTHOR

Kathleen Corrigan moved from elementary teaching to children's book writing to share wonder with young readers. Her adventures have taken her around the world—from tasting Moroccan street food to SCUBA diving Australia's Great Barrier Reef, searching for the Loch Ness Monster, and learning "thank you" in many languages (often amusing locals). With Antarctica and penguin encounters next on her list, she dreams of going to space and writing a book while there. Until then, she continues creating stories from every corner of Earth.

Table of Contents

AS YOU READ, LOOK FOR **CONSONANT BLENDS**

CHAPTER 1

Meet Some Monster Machines

Have you ever seen a machine as big as a house? In this book, you will meet huge machines made of steel and other metals.

These giant machines smash rocks, drill spots, and lift things as big as ten trucks. Some seem to stand as tall as the sky. Others stretch as long as six buses.

When we plan to build big things, we need strong machines to help. They dig in the ground, help rockets lift to space, and swim in the sea.

Black smoke may puff from their **stacks** as they work. Glass windows and slick metal parts gleam in the sun. Some machines are so big that workers can sleep and eat inside them!

These machines help us in many ways in our daily routines. They can scoop up dirt and swing huge blocks to make tall buildings. These machines can lift heavy objects that people and small trucks can't move.

These giants make a lot of noise! They clank and grind as they work. The ground may shake when they move past. But they get big jobs done fast. Get set to see the biggest, strongest, and coolest machines ever made!

Tractors can be very small or as big as this one! These wheels stand taller than the boy on the step.

BAGGER 293: THE LAND GIANT

When we need to dig huge holes or lift heavy things, we need special machines. Let's meet three of the most amazing ones.

The Bagger 293 is the biggest land vehicle ever created! It stands 315 feet (96 meters) tall. That's as high as a 30-story skyscraper! This machine weighs over 31 million pounds (over 14 million kilograms). That's as much as 9,000 big elephants all stacked up!

The Bagger is long, too. It is as long as two football fields. The Bagger runs on special tracks. But it goes very slowly—slower than you walk. Its strong metal parts gleam in the sun.

This huge digger works in coal mines in Germany. Its job is to scoop up dirt to find coal under the ground. The wheel on its arm has big buckets that can fill many trucks with just one spin.

Workers climb up long steps inside the machine to get to their jobs. They help control the giant arm that digs into the ground. The fresh dirt drops with a plunk as it falls onto trucks below.

The Bagger can dig as much dirt in a day as 40,000 workers with shovels would dig.

When the Bagger moves, the ground shakes and trembles!

BERTHA: THE TUNNEL MAKER

Bertha was one of the biggest tunnel-making machines ever built. Her job was to dig a huge tunnel under the city of Seattle.

This big digger had a round face that spun and cut through dirt and rock. The face was as wide as a street with five cars side by side. As Bertha drilled forward, she left a tunnel big enough for cars to drive through.

Workers stood inside Bertha to run her. The machine didn't just dig—it also put up walls to keep the tunnel strong as it went. It was like digging and building at the same time.

Bertha's task was to make a space for cars to drive without having to stop at lights. Sprinklers kept the dust down as she dug.

The front of Bertha was built to cut through hard rock and soft sand. Special tools on her face could grind up huge stones into small bits.

Bertha had to stop sometimes when she got stuck. Once, she was stuck for almost a year! Crews had to dig a deep shaft from the street to fix her.

When Bertha finished her job, she had dug a tunnel almost two miles (three kilometers) long. The **drill bits** were left behind, but her control room was lifted out and saved.

It took almost four years to build the tunnel under Seattle.

A COLOSSAL CRANE

The Liebherr (LEEB-hayr) LR 13000 is one of the tallest cranes in the world. It can stretch higher than a ten-story building.

This giant crane stands on wide tracks so that it doesn't sink into soft ground. It can lift things as heavy as 30 city buses. That's more than a jumbo jet airliner!

The crane is too big and slow to drive to work. It comes in many bits on lots of trucks. Workers spend days putting it back together.

The crane spins to pick up heavy loads and set them down again in the right place. It helps build bridges, power plants, and other big structures.

The crane must stay very still when lifting. If it tilts or slips, it could drop its load. Each lift is carefully planned by skilled workers.

Strong **cables** hang from the top. They lift steel beams and concrete blocks high into the air. From far away, the cables look like string. But they are thick and strong.

When a storm comes, the crane must stop. Wind can push it and make it sway or shake.

DID YOU KNOW?
The weight on the back of the crane is as heavy as 1,500 cars. It keeps the crane from tipping over.

The crane's long arms are even longer than an Olympic swimming pool!

CHAPTER 3

Mega Movers

THE CATERPILLAR 797F: A MONSTER TRUCK

The Caterpillar 797F is a giant truck. Its wheels stand taller than two grown-ups stacked up on top of each other.

This monster works in mines carrying rocks filled with gold, copper, and other metals. It can haul as much rock as 13 concrete mixer trucks. Its dump bed is so big, a pickup truck would fit in it with space left over.

The driver must climb a step ladder to get to the cab. From this height, they look down upon regular cars that seem like small toys. The steering wheel looks like a car's, but everything else is much, much bigger.

Its engine is as strong as a freight train. It drinks over 100 gallons (378 liters) of fuel every hour when working hard. Black smoke puffs from its stacks as it rumbles and grinds up steep slopes.

The truck has six huge wheels with special treads. Each tire can cost more than a brand-new car. If one goes flat, a special team must bring in cranes to lift the truck and fix it.

Even when it's empty, this truck weighs more than 100 cars. When it's full of rocks, it becomes one of the heaviest land vehicles on the planet!

CATERPILLAR
202
202

NASA'S CRAWLER-TRANSPORTER: THE ROCKET MOVER

NASA's crawler-transporter looks like a giant, flat platform on tracks. Its job is to carry space rockets to the launchpads.

This **massive** machine creeps slowly like a snail does. It must go slowly because the rocket is tall and heavy. If it moves too fast, it could tip or shake the rocket!

The crawler-transporter has eight tracks (like the ones on tanks). Each track has 57 metal shoes. Those are the bits that touch the ground. The tracks help spread the weight out so the crawler-transporter doesn't sink into the sand.

It takes a team of 30 people to drive and control the crawler-transporter. The driver sits in a cab at one corner of the platform. They must be very careful not to bump into or tilt the rocket!

The crawler-transporter can move itself both up and down like a giant elevator. When it picks up a rocket and its launch tower, the crawler-transporter must stay perfectly flat. This is to keep everything safe and steady.

This giant transporter only goes 42 feet (12 meters) per gallon of fuel. That's like using a whole car's gas tank just to drive from a front door to the street!

The crawler-transporter slowly creeps along the ground.

PIONEERING SPIRIT: GIANT OF THE SEA

Pioneering Spirit is the biggest work ship in the world. It looks like a giant aircraft carrier split down the middle with a big gap in the front.

This massive ship was built to lift an oil platform off the sea, or to place one there. Oil platforms are huge metal structures where workers drill for oil deep under the ocean. *Pioneering Spirit* can also help install wind farms at sea.

The ship is almost as long as ten swimming pools placed end-to-end. It has room for 571 people to sleep, eat, and work while at sea. The ship even has its own hospital, gym, and movie theater.

Pioneering Spirit has a special trick. It can slide under a platform, then lift the whole thing in one piece! When it lifts a platform, big lifter beams reach out from both sides of the ship. These beams grab hold of the platform from below, then slowly raise it out of the water.

The ship must stay very still while lifting or lowering. And if big waves come, it must wait for calm weather conditions. Special computers help keep it steady. They use powerful thrusters that can spin in any direction.

Pioneering Spirit can lift as much as 48,000 tons. That's like picking up 300 jumbo jets at once!

CHAPTER

4

Amazing Machines for Science

LARGE HADRON COLLIDER: THE RING UNDER THE GROUND

Some giant machines help us learn about our world and the tiny bits that make it up!

The Large Hadron Collider (LHC) is shaped like a giant ring. It's buried deep underground between Switzerland and France. The ring is so big that it would take you more than an hour to walk all the way around it!

Inside the ring, tiny **particles** zoom around almost at the speed of light! The machine smashes these particles together to see what they're made of. When they crash, they break into smaller pieces. Scientists study these pieces to learn how the universe works.

The LHC uses powerful magnets that are colder than space. This is meant to keep the particles on track. These magnets are so strong they could lift a battleship! Supercomputers help scientists see when the particles hit each other and explode into bits.

This machine helped scientists discover the **Higgs boson**, or the "God particle." It helps explain why things have mass, or why objects weigh something.

Though we can't see it from above ground, the LHC helps us understand our world. From stars and planets to light, gravity, and the tiniest parts of matter, it teaches us about many things.

The LHC is a huge and very complex machine.

JAMES WEBB SPACE TELESCOPE: A GOLDEN EYE IN SPACE

The James Webb Space Telescope is the biggest space telescope ever built. It looks like a giant gold mirror with a sun shield the size of a tennis court.

This amazing telescope sits far from Earth—about a million miles away! It took a whole month for the telescope to travel that far after it was launched. This telescope can see deep into the universe without light from Earth getting in the way.

The telescope must stay very cold to work properly. Its gold mirrors help it see heat from faraway stars and planets. A giant sun shield blocks heat from the Sun, Earth, and Moon. This keeps the mirrors colder than ice cream in a freezer.

Scientists use Webb to study planets around other stars. It can even tell if a planet has water or air just by studying the light coming from it.

Unlike giant machines on Earth, Webb is not very heavy. It had to be light enough to fly on a rocket. In space, it slowly unfolded like a giant piece of **origami**. There were over 300 steps and every move had to be perfect. If not, the telescope wouldn't work at all.

So far, Webb has found galaxies farther away than any detected before. It's like having a time machine that lets us peek into the very beginning of the universe!

The James Webb Space Telescope observes the universe.

The Observing Side of the James Webb Space Telescope

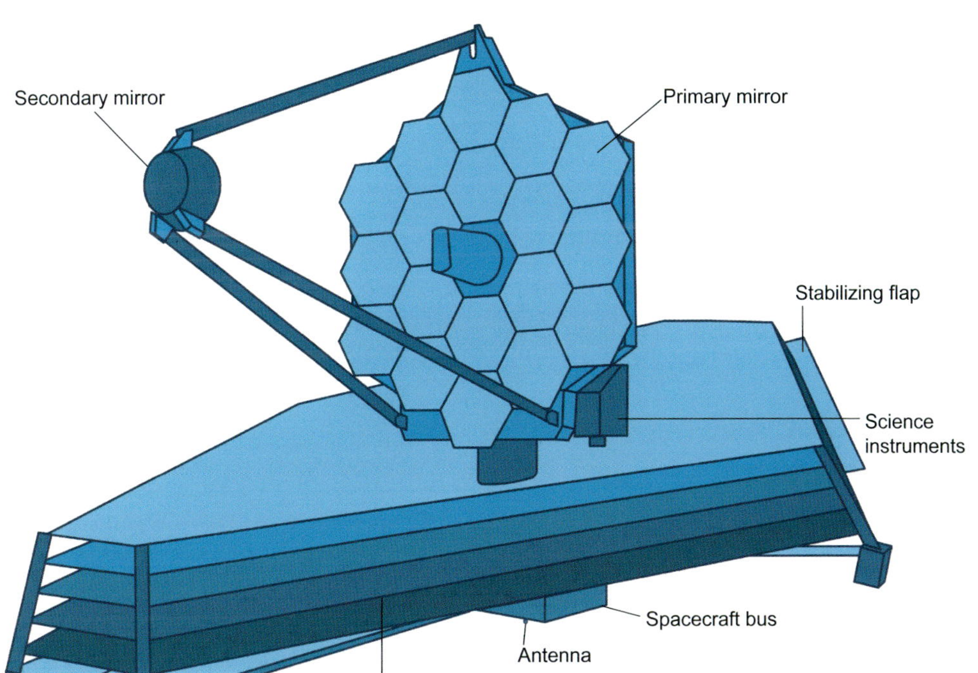

ROOM-SIZED BRAINS: EARLY COMPUTERS

The first computers were enormous machines that filled entire rooms! In the 1940s and 1950s, computers like the ENIAC were as big as three school buses.

These huge thinking machines had many glass vacuum tubes that glowed because they got hot. The tubes would often break and had to be replaced. A single calculation might take several seconds to complete.

Early computers needed special cooling systems because they got very hot. The rooms had to stay cold, and workers often wore sweaters, even in summer!

To program these computers, people had to plug in wires and flip switches. There were no screens or keyboards like we have today. The computer would print out its answers on paper.

By the 1960s, computers advanced even more with spinning magnetic tapes and disks. These big flat disks stored information and spun very fast. Sometimes workers wore special clean clothes and masks to keep dust off the computer parts. Even a tiny speck of dust could make the computer stop working!

The computer rooms had special floors that let cool air flow up from underneath. This stopped the machines from getting too warm.

These massive machines weighed several tons and had to be built on strong floors. Despite their size, they were less powerful than the small phones we use today!

The giant computers of the 1960s had many parts.

SUPERCOMPUTERS TODAY: GIGANTIC POWER

Today's supercomputers are much smaller than the first computers were. But they can do so much more! These machines fill big rooms with rows of tall, black cabinets.

Inside the cabinets are thousands of small computers working together. Miles of cables connect them so they can share information fast. These machines can do trillions of calculations every second!

Supercomputers need special cooling systems because they get very hot. Many companies use water pipes that run next to the computer parts to keep them cool. Some companies even use the exact same kind of cooling liquid that's inside your refrigerator.

Scientists have many uses for supercomputers. They can predict weather, design new medicines, and study stars and planets. Other scientists model what could happen during storms or earthquakes to keep people safe.

The fastest supercomputers in the world have funny names like Frontier and Summit. They use as much electricity as a small town and cost millions of dollars to build. Teams of computer experts work together both day and night to keep them running.

DID YOU KNOW?

Scientists are now building a new kind of machine called a quantum computer. These use tiny particles smaller than atoms! Regular computers use 1s and 0s. A quantum computer uses qubits, which can be both 1 and 0 at the same time. They could rapidly solve problems that would otherwise take thousands of years!

What Makes These Giants Go?

ELECTRICITY

Bagger 293
Powers 50,000 homes

Bertha
Powers giant drill

Computers
Need cooling fans

LHC
Powers magnets

Supercomputers
Power a town

DIESEL FUEL

Crane
100 gallons/day

Caterpillar
Huge fuel tank

Crawler-Transporter
42 feet/gallon

Pioneering Spirit
Months of fuel

 SOLAR POWER

James Webb
Power from Sun

CHAPTER 5

The Silliest Giant Machines

RUBE GOLDBERG: MASTER OF CRAZY CONTRAPTIONS

Rube Goldberg wasn't a builder. He was a cartoonist who drew funny pictures. In the 1920s, he started drawing strange machines that did simple jobs in silly ways.

His machines might use 20 steps just to wipe your nose or crack an egg! One famous drawing shows the pulling of a string that makes a bird fly out. This tips a cup, spilling water onto a plant and causing it to grow quickly. The growth pushes a ball that turns on a switch—all just to scratch someone's back!

Rube never built these crazy **contraptions** himself. He just drew them to make people laugh. His name became famous for these silly machines. Today we still call them "Rube Goldberg machines."

DID YOU KNOW?

Some schools have contests for students to build their own Rube Goldberg machines. Try making one at home using toys, books, marbles, and any other items you might find.

People loved Rube's wild ideas so much that they started building real versions of them. Contests emerged asking people to create the funniest, craziest machines that might actually work.

These machines may not be big in size, but they are giants in the number of steps they take. Some use balls rolling down tracks. Others use springs bouncing and dominoes falling. All actions are connected together in one long chain reaction.

Self-Operating Napkin

One of Rube Goldberg's machines was invented to help wipe your mouth!

MODERN RUBE GOLDBERG MACHINES: BIG IN STEPS IF NOT IN SIZE

Today, people build Rube Goldberg machines that have a lot of steps! Rube's original drawings might have had up to 20 steps. In comparison, modern machines can have hundreds.

Purdue University holds a famous Rube Goldberg Machine Contest each year. Students spend months planning and building machines with at least 75 steps. These machines do simple tasks like putting a stamp on an envelope or watering a plant.

In 2012, one team built a 300-step machine just to blow up and pop a balloon! It took six months to plan and two months to build. The machine filled a whole room. It contained tracks, swings, levers, and pulleys that all worked together.

The Guinness World Record for one of these machines is held by a Latvian business. 4Fun is the name of their company. Their machine had 412 steps and took 571 tries to work perfectly from start to finish!

These machines are special because each step must trigger the next in a perfect chain. If just one part fails, the whole system fails. That's why builders plan carefully and test each section again and again.

GIGANTIC MACHINES: FROM MASSIVE TO MARVELOUS

We've traveled from the big diggers to tiny computer parts. We have encountered machines that weigh tons to ones that float in space.

All these machines show how humans can solve big problems with clever thinking. These machines can lift heavy loads, dig tunnels, explore space, or make us laugh. Gigantic machines help us do things we could never do on our own!

err LR 13000

Giant computer, 1960s

CONSONANT BLEND WORD LISTS

l-blends

black
blocks
blow
clank
clean
clever
climb
clothes
flat
flip
float
floors
flow
fly
glass
gleam
glowed
place(d)(s)
plan
planet(s)
planned
planning
plant(s)
platform(s)
plug
plunk

r-blends

brains
brand
break
bridges
bring
crack
crane(s)
crash
crawler
craziest
crazy
cream
create(d)
creeps
crews
drawing(s)
drew
drill(ed)
drinks
drive(r)
drop(s)
France
freezer
freight
fresh
from
front
frontier
grab
gravity
grind(s)
ground
grow(n)(th)
predict
print
problems
program
properly
track(s)
tractors
train
transporter
traveled
treads
trembles
trick
tries
trigger
trillions
truck(s)
try

s-blends

school(s)
scoop
scratches
screens
skilled
sky(scraper)
sleep
slick
slides
slips
slopes
slow(s)(er)(ly)
small(er)
smash(es)
smoke
snail
space
special
speck
speed
spend
spent
spilling
spin(ning)(s)
spirit
split
spots
spread
springs
sprinklers
spun
stacked
stacks
stamp
stand(s)
stars
start(ed)
stay
steady
steel
steep
steering
step(s)
still
stones
stood
stop(ped)(ping)(s)
stored
storm(s)
story
strange
street
stretch(es)
string

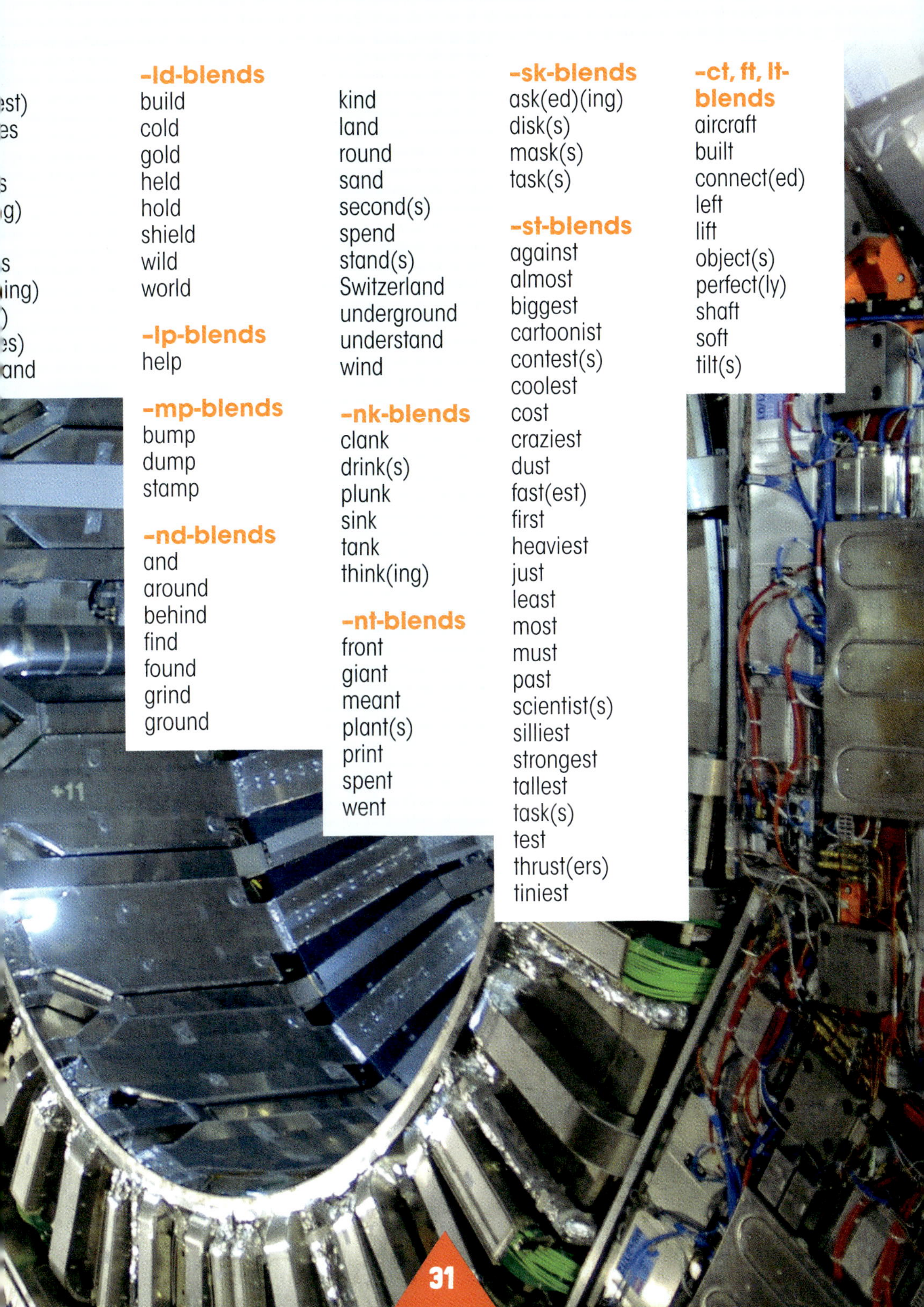

est)
es

s
g)

s
ing)
)
es)
and

-ld-blends
build
cold
gold
held
hold
shield
wild
world

-lp-blends
help

-mp-blends
bump
dump
stamp

-nd-blends
and
around
behind
find
found
grind
ground
kind
land
round
sand
second(s)
spend
stand(s)
Switzerland
underground
understand
wind

-nk-blends
clank
drink(s)
plunk
sink
tank
think(ing)

-nt-blends
front
giant
meant
plant(s)
print
spent
went

-sk-blends
ask(ed)(ing)
disk(s)
mask(s)
task(s)

-st-blends
against
almost
biggest
cartoonist
contest(s)
coolest
cost
craziest
dust
fast(est)
first
heaviest
just
least
most
must
past
scientist(s)
silliest
strongest
tallest
task(s)
test
thrust(ers)
tiniest

-ct, ft, lt-blends
aircraft
built
connect(ed)
left
lift
object(s)
perfect(ly)
shaft
soft
tilt(s)

GLOSSARY

cables (KAY-buls): thick, strong ropes made of steel or fiber

contraptions (kun-TRAP-shunz): gadgets or devices, often with a strange design

drill bits (DRILL BITS): tools to cut holes

Higgs boson (HIGZ BOH-sun): a basic particle that gives mass to other particles

massive (MAS-iv): enormous and heavy

origami (or-ih-GAH-mee): Japanese paper-folding art

particles (PAR-ti-kulz): units for building blocks or units of matter or energy

quantum computer (KWAN-tum kom-PYOO-ter): a new approach to computing that is much faster

qubits (KYOO-bits): short for quantum bits; the basic (smallest) units of information

stacks (STAKS): chimneys

INDEX